Colour Meditation

Timelessness

White

The soul is created in a place
between Time and Eternity:
with its highest powers it touches Eternity,
with its lower Time.

Meister Eckhart

The Tree of Eternity has its roots above
And its branches on earth below.

The Katha Upanishad

This place
where you are right now,
God circled on a map
for you.

Hafiz

Step out of
the circle of time
And into the circle
of love.

Rumi

In love, aside from sipping the wine of timelessness,
Nothing else exists.
There is no reason for living except for giving one's life.
I said, "First I know you, then I die."
He said, "For the one who knows Me, there is no dying."

Rumi

Firstness and lastness pertain to the contingent world and not
to the world of God. For God the beginning and end are one
and the same... Likewise, the Word of God is sanctified above all
these conditions and exalted beyond every law, constraint,
or limitation that may exist in the contingent world.

'Abdu'l-Bahá

O God, create in the hearts of Thy beloved the fire of Thy love,
that it may consume the thought of everything save Thee.

Reveal to us, Thine exalted eternity -
that Thou hast ever been and wilt ever be.

Bahá'u'lláh

Most humbly we bow to You, O Supreme Lord.
At Your command moves the mighty wheel of time.
You are eternal, and beyond eternity.

Artharva Veda

Give me a new life
at every instant
and bestow upon me
the breaths
of the Holy spirit
at every moment

Abdu'l-Bahá

Let thine everlasting melodies breathe tranquillity on me

— Bahá'u'lláh

More and more I find I want to be living

in a Big Here and a Long

N   o   w

There is only
one time
when it is
essential
to awaken.
That time is

NOW

Jack Kornfield

Don't cry over the past;
it's gone.
Don't stress about the future;
it hasn't arrived.
Live in the present
and make it beautiful.

Ida Scott Taylor

You must live in the present,
launch yourself on every wave,
find your eternity in each moment

Henry David Thoreau

Most humans are never fully present in the now,
because unconsciously they believe
that the next moment
must be more important than this one.
But then you miss your whole life,
which is never not now.

Eckart Tolle

All you really need to do
is accept this moment fully.
You are then at ease in the here and now
and at ease with yourself.

Eckart Tolle

That moment when this heart.. stops..
almost as if it never existed.

When every.. breath.. slows down..
almost as if you never ... needed a single breath of air.

When time stops.. almost as if every second never mattered.

In that moment... I'm infinite.

In that moment... I am immortal.

In that moment... I am Finally alive.

Hafsa Shah

Close your eyes and you will see clearly,
Cease to listen and you will hear the truth,
Be silent and your heart will sing.

Taoist Meditation

Ease the pounding of my heart
by the quieting of my mind.

Steady my hurried pace with a vision
of the eternal reach of time.

Orin L. Crain

What a wonderful thing it would be
If once a day
The path of our fleeting lives
And the river of eternal time
Could intersect
So we might sit on the bank
And just watch the water flow.

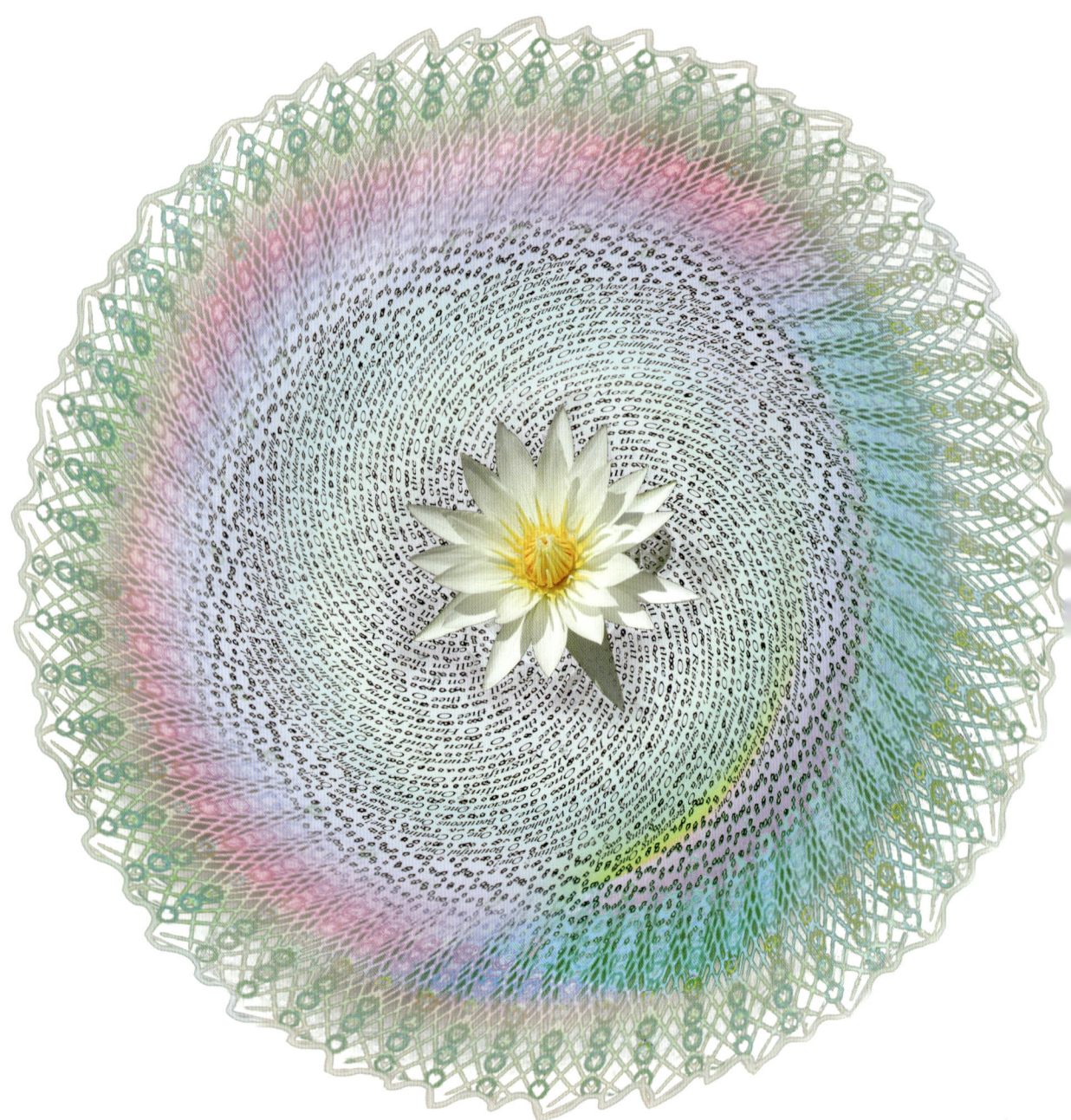

If you feel lost, disappointed, hesitant, or weak, return to yourself, to who you are, here and now and when you get there, you will discover yourself, like a lotus flower in full bloom, even in a muddy pond, beautiful and strong.

Masaru Emoto

O mind, love the Lord,
As the lotus loves the water.
Tossed about by the waves,
It still blossoms with love.

Sri Guru Granth Sahib Ji

Imagine that the universe is a great spinning engine. You want to stay near the core of the thing - right in the hub of the wheel - not out at the edges where all the wild whirling takes place, where you can get frayed and crazy. The hub of calmness - that's your heart. That's where God lives within you. So stop looking for answers in the world. Just keep coming back to that centre and you'll always find peace.

Elizabeth Gilbert

FEBRUARY

MARCH

APRIL

MAY

JUNE

JULY

24

Time is the result of change
and not by the movement of planets and stars.
Hence time is timeless.

Bhagavad Gita

The little space within the heart
is as great as the vast universe.
The heavens and the earth are there,
and the sun and the moon and the stars.
Fire and lightning and winds are there,
and all that now is and all that is not.

Swami Prabhavananda

Dost thou reckon thyself only a puny form
When within thee the universe is folded?

Imám 'Ali

Whatever happens to you
has been waiting to happen
since the beginning of time.

The twining strands of fate
wove both of them together:
your own existence and
the things that happen to you.

To love only
what happens,
what was destined.
No greater harmony.

Marcus Aurelius

The spirit, without moving, is swifter than the mind;
the senses cannot reach him: he is ever beyond them.

Isa Upanishad

The human soul is exalted above all egress and regress.
It is still, and yet it soareth; it moveth, and yet it is still.
It is, in itself, a testimony that beareth witness
to the existence of a world that is contingent,
as well as to the reality of a world
that hath neither beginning nor end.

Blessed is the one who discovereth the fragrance of
inner meanings from the traces of this Pen through
whose movement the breezes of God are wafted over
the entire creation, and through whose stillness the very
essence of tranqillity appeareth in the realm of being.

Baha'u'llah

A single moment
of awakening
in this world

Is eternity
in the world
to come.

The inner peace
of the world to come

Is living in this world
with full attention.

The two are one,
flip sides of a coin

forever tumbling
and never caught.

Pirke Avot

Your existence, O love my dear
Has been sealed and marked

"Too sacred," "too sacred" by the Beloved-
To ever end!

Indeed God
Has written a thousand promises
All over your heart

That say,
Life, life, life
Is far too sacred to
Ever end.

Hafiz

In a boat down a fast-running creek,
It feels like trees on the bank
Are rushing by. What seems

To be changing around us
Is rather the speed of our craft
Leaving this world.

Rumi

Write down my name with the names of them who,
from eternity, have circled round the Tabernacle of Thy majesty,
and clung to the hem of Thy loving-kindness,
and held fast the cord of Thy tender mercy.

Bahá'u'lláh

The world is the wheel of God, turning round
and round with all living creatures upon the wheel.
The world is the river of God,
Flowing from him and flowing back to him.

On this ever-revolving wheel of life
The individual self goes round and round
Through life after life, believing itself to be a separate creature,
until it sees its identity with the Lord of Love
and attains immortality in the indivisible Whole.

The Shvetashvatara Upanishad

We have to make our practice the shape of a circle.
A circle never comes to an end. Keep it going continually.

Anon

To travel a circle is to journey over the same ground time
and time again. To travel a circle wisely is to journey over
the same ground for the first time. In this way, the ordinary
becomes extraordinary, and the circle, a path to where you
wish to be. And when you notice at last that the path has
circled back into itself, you realize that where you wish to be
is where you have already been ... and always were.

Neale Donald Walsch

We shall not cease from exploration
And the end of all our exploring
Will be to arrive where we started
And know the place for the first time.

T.S. Eliot

…and the sands in the glass
Stopped
For a pure white moment
While gravity sprinkled upward
Like rain, rising.

Mary Oliver

All Heaven and Earth
Flowered white obliterate...
Snow...unceasing snow.

Hashin

Mind set free in the Dharma-realm
I sit at the moon filled window
Watching the mountains with my ears,
Hearing the stream with open eyes.
Each molecule preaches perfect law,
Each moment chants true sutra;
The most fleeting thought is timeless,
A single hair's enough to stir the sea.

Shutaku

How fortunate are you and I
whose home is timelessness.

We who have wandered down
from fragrant mountains of Now.

E.E. Cummings

The snow goose need not bathe
to make itself white.

Neither need you do anything
but be yourself.

Lao-Tse

Seizing my life in your hands,
you thrash it clean

On the savage rocks
of Eternal Mind.

How its colours bled,
until they grew white!

You smile and sit back;
I dry in your sun.

Rumi

This is how it always is when I finish a poem.

A great silence overcomes me

And I wonder why

I ever thought

to use language.

Rumi

REFERENCES

p. 2.   **Image: Mansion of Mazra'ih**

p. 3a   Meister Eckhart, www.azquotes.com

p. 3b   *The Katha Upanishad, Timeless Wisdom,* Eknath Easwaran. Nilgiri Press, 2008, p190

p. 4.   Hafiz, *Translation by Daniel Ladinsky, The Subject Tonight is Love,* Compass, 2003.

p. 5.   Jalalu'd-Din Rumi, www.goodreads.com

p. 7.   Rumi, Translatons by Shahram Shiva, *Rumi, Thief of Sleep* (wwww.allpoetry.com)

p. 9a.   Bahá'u'lláh, *Bahá'í Prayers,* Bahá'í Publishing Trust UK, Rutland Gate, 1975, p.61

p. 9b   *Artharva Veda, Hinduism,* www.chaplaincyinstitute.org

p. 10.   'Abdu'l-Bahá, *Prayer for Steadfastness,* www.bahai-libuary.com

p. 11.   Bahá'u'lláh, *Bahá'í Prayers,* Bahá'í Publishing Trust, Wilmette, Illinois, 2002, pp.164-165

p. 12.   Brian Eno, www.goodreads.com

p. 13.   Jack Kornfield, Buddha's little instruction book, New York: Bantam, 1994

p. 14a   Adapted from Ida Scott Taylor, www.goodreads.com/quotes/8858-do-not-back-and-grieve-over-the-past-for

p. 14b   Henry David Thoreau, hdt.typepad.com/henrys_blog/2010/04/april-24-1859.html

p. 15a   Eckart Tolle, www.the guardian.com/books/2009/apr/11/eckart-tolle-interview-spirituality

p. 15b   Eckart Tolle, *Practicing the Power of Now: Essential Teachings, Meditations and Exercises from the Power of Now,* www.goodreads.com

p. 17.   Hafsa Shah, www.goodreads.com

p. 19a   Taoist Meditation, www.davar.net/ZEN/ENTRACTS.HTM

p. 19b   Orin L. Crain, *One Hundred ways to Serenity,* Celia Haddon, Hoddera & Stoughton, 1998, p.7

p. 21.   Source Unknown

p. 23a   Masaru Emoto, *Secret Life of Water,* www.goodreads.com

p. 23b   Sri Guru Granth Shib Ji, www.rajkaregakhalsa.net/Guarbani/Amrit/164 html

p. 23c   Elizabeth Gilbert, *The Complete Elizabeth Gilbert: Eat, Pray,Love.* A & C Black, 2010, p217

p. 25a   *Bhagavad Gita,* Source Unknown

p. 25b   Swami Prabhavananda, *The Upanishads: Breath from the Eternal.*

p. 25c   Imám 'Ali. Quoted by Báha'u'lláh in *The Seven Valleys*, US. Publishing Trust, 1991, p. 34

pp. 26-7. Marcus Aurelius, *Meditations: A New Translation*, 10:5, Random House Publishing Group, 2002, p132

p. 29a   *Isa Upanishad 4, Sacred Scriptures of the World Religions, An introduction,* John Price, A & C Black, 2010

p. 29b   Bahá'u'lláh, *Gleanings from the Writings of Bahá'u'lláh,* US Baha'i Publishing Trust, 1990 pocket-size edition, LXXXII: p.161-2

p. 29c   Bahá'u'lláh, *Kitáb-i-Aqdas,* Bahá'í World Centre, 1992, p76

pp. 30-1. Pirke Avot 4:22, *The Essential Mystics,* Andrew Harvey, Castle Books, 1996, p.102

p. 32.   Hafiz, *The Gift, Translations by Daniel Ladinsky,* Penguin Compass, 1999, p.81

p. 33.   Rumi, *The Essential Rumi, Translated by Coleman Barks,* Penguin Books, 1995, p.194

p. 35a   Bahá'u'lláh, Prayers and Meditations, US Bahá'í Publishing Trust, 1987, XVIII, p.21

p. 35b   *Shvetashvatara 1.4-6, The Upanishads: The Classics of Indian Spirituality,* Ekhath Easwaran, xli, Read How You Want.com, 2010

p. 37a   Source Unknown

p. 37b   Neale Donald Walsch, *The New Revelations: A Conversation with God.* Hachette UK. 2010

p. 37c   T.S. Eliot, *Little Gidding, T.S. Eliot, The Poems,* Martin Scofield, Cambridge University Press. 1988.

p. 39a   Mary Oliver, *Owls and Other fantasies: Poems and Essays. Such Singing in the Wild Branches.* Beacon Press, 2006

p. 39b   Hashin, *Japanese Haiku,* Peter Beilenson, Library of Alexandria.

p. 40   **Image: Adapted from photograph by Thomas Pavlasek/ Myslite/Dreamstime.com-Frosty Morning Photo**

p. 41a   Shutaku, *The Essentail Mystics,* Andrew Harvey, Castle Books, 1996, p.85

p. 41b   E.E.Cummings, *E.E. Cummings By Catherine Reef,* Houghton Mifflin Harcourt, 2006

p. 43a   Lao-Tse, *The Reconnection by Eric Pearl,* Read How You Want.com, 2011, p197

p. 43b   Rumi, *The Essential Mystics, Andrew Harvey.* Castle Books, 1996, p161

p. 44   Rumi, *The Essential Rumi, Translated by Coleman Barks,* Penguin Books, 1995, p.20

First Published in the UK in 2017 by
Intellect, The Mill, Parnall Road, Fishponds, Bristol, BS16 3JG, UK

A catalogue record for this book is available from the British Library.

Book Design: Corinne Randall
Publisher: Masoud Yazdani
ISBN 978-1-78320-800-5
Printed and bound by Gomer Press.

Distributor: Stephen Vickers, 2 Glovers Close, Woodstock, Oxfordshire, OX20 1NS, UK
www.corinnerandall.co.uk

MIX
Paper from
responsible sources
FSC
www.fsc.org
FSC® C114687

Colour Meditations

Timelessness : White

Paradise : Purple

Flight : Blue

The Ocean : Turquoise

Nature : Green

Light : Yellow

Joy : Orange

Adoration : Red

Mystery : Black